49 USES FOR A WALKING STICK

For Stackridge – the sorely underrated West Country band who opened the very first Glastonbury Festival in 1970. Their 1976 release *Mr. Mick* is unique in the pantheon of bizarre concept albums in that it is the only one that prominently features a walking stick.

First published in the United Kingdom in 2018 by National Trust Books, 43 Great Ormond Street, London WC1N 3HZ. An imprint of Pavilion Books Group Ltd.
© National Trust Books, 2018

Inside illustrations by Peter James Field

ISBN: 978-1-911358-74-9

Repro by Rival Colour Ltd, UK. Printed by 1010 Printing International Ltd, China | 10 9 8 7 6 5 4 3 2 1

This book is of a light-hearted nature, and though appearing to be a practical, how-to guide, is intended as a whimsical diversion. The walking stick user is not advised to emulate the uses described in this book. Please use your walking stick responsibly!

49
USES
FOR A
WALKING
STICK

**FRANK
HOPKINSON**

 National Trust

Introduction

If someone invented the walking stick today it would probably win awards and have pride of place in London's Design Museum. The variety of uses it can be applied to are so numerous they make inventor James Dyson look like Hengist Pod from *Carry On Cleo*, the character who cycled everywhere on his square-wheeled bike.

The walking stick is the original multi-tool. Take one wherever you go and you are equipped to perform many different and fascinating tasks. And unlike a Swiss Army penknife, you won't lose a fingernail trying to lever it into action.

For the purposes of uniformity we have used the classic, old-school, wooden-handled walking stick in our illustrations, sometimes flouting Health and Safety conventions by removing the rubber tip. Other specialist walking sticks are available, including hiking poles and the ingenious folding walking stick, which splits into sections (not to be used for any task requiring serious leverage).

We have limited ourselves to just 49 different applications, but of course there are many more, some at the more abstract end of the spectrum. For example, combined with a dangled carrot, it can provide 50 per cent of a motivational package. It is also a dangerous weapon of mischief. The old gag of tapping somebody on the shoulder from the other side can be extended a lot further with a walking stick, especially in a crowded lift.

In Victorian England it was almost *de rigueur* for gents to stroll around town equipped with a suitable walking stick. Given the current trend of reviving old things we thought had been consigned to fashion museums – such as scooters, beards and vinyl records – it can only be a matter of time before hipsters are sporting elegant walking sticks, while Urban Outfitters will be keen to stock a variety of retro models. This is what they can be used for ...

Frank Hopkinson is the author of two popular miscellanies, *The Joy of Sheds* and *The Joy of Pubs*. A former Butlin's press officer, his debut novel, *The Last Resort* (2019) depicts the 1983 summer season at Clacton-on-Sea.

Insect investigation lever

While out walking in the countryside it's fun to lift a large rock and observe Mother Nature at work underneath. This can take many forms: a disgruntled amphibian who has found a secure nook in which to rest while waiting for wetter weather, or the intricate architecture of an ant colony with its myriad chambers and purposeful activity. Lifting up sizeable objects is not easy, but a walking stick makes the perfect lever. First find a smaller stone to act as a fulcrum; placing that close to the rock, jam one end of the stick underneath the selected slab. Apply what physicists would call an 'input force' at the handle end. The walking stick will amplify the effort to produce a far greater output force and lift the rock. Pay attention to any fauna that might be crushed on the rock's sudden return to its start position.

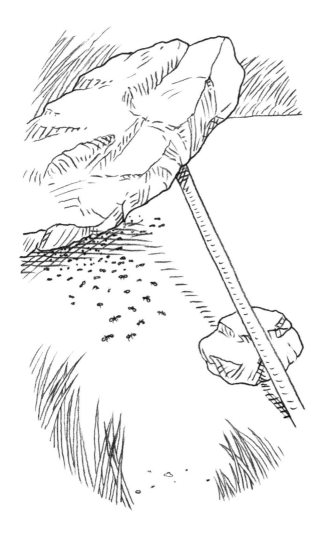

Puddle depth tester

Sometimes, while out on a countryside footpath, one can encounter an enormous puddle that blocks the way. If you don't have a dog or a small child to send on ahead, it's difficult to gauge its depth. You have to ask yourself the perennial question – 'Is it a wellington topper?' Experience may tell you that terra firma lies just a few inches beneath that opaque brown surface, but it is wise to assume nothing. Use your walking stick to probe that puddle and ascertain the depth in various places . Although a quick visual assessment of the depth your stick has submerged is usually enough, those with a more scientific disposition may want to calibrate their walking stick in some way. Should your walking stick go in all the way up to the handle, then you have found a sink hole.

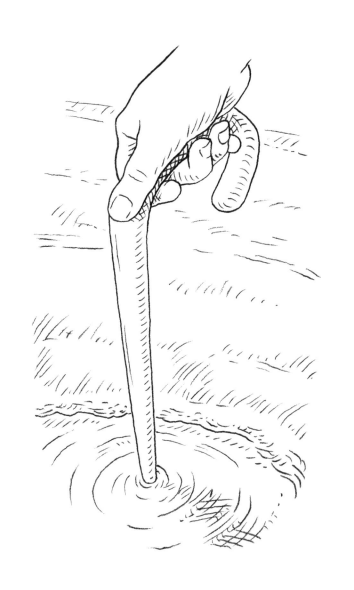

Low-hanging fruit collector

Gardening experts suggest that the right time to pick a fruit is when it can be held in the hand so that a gentle twist will separate stalk from branch. However, gently cupping some ripe fruit is not possible when it's eight feet in the air. Not unless you have a walking stick. Two methods can be used: the fruit can be brought lower using the handle to hook over the branch and draw it down; or else give the fruit a quick hoick and be ready to catch it with your free hand when it falls. In both cases it is important to hold on tightly to the walking stick in case it is suddenly whipped back by the recoil action of the branch, sending your stick springing high into the tree. That would be nothing short of embarrassing.

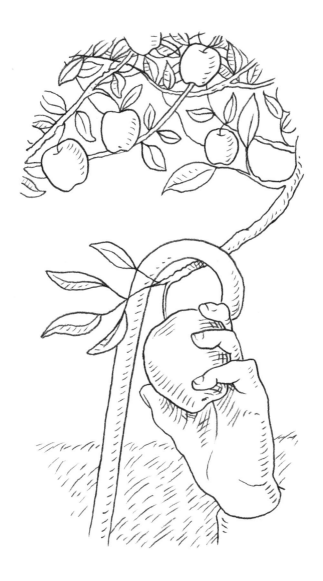

Nettle swisher

A walking stick can play a valuable part in contributing to countryside maintenance. At the height of summer, plants grow quickly and even the most regularly used footpath can be overwhelmed by marauding growth from hedgerow plants. Goosegrass, cow parsley, thistles and – worst of all – nettles can all be beaten back with a hearty blow from a well-aimed walking stick to clear the way. Brambles are a tougher proposition, but an accurate blow can often remove the growing tip. A bold forehand or backhand swishing action should be used depending on personal preference, though combining the two will engage more muscle groups. Apart from helping clear the way, vigorous and sustained nettle swishing offers a great opportunity for aerobic exercise.

Dead animal
sign-of-life tester

Is it or isn't it? The eternal question when
faced with a motionless animal in an unexpected
location. Has it stunned itself momentarily? Is it
asleep? Is it dormant? Is it an old sponge that the
light has caught in a particular way to make it look
like an animal? Being kind and curious, you want
to resolve the situation by seeing if there are signs
of life. Perhaps if it's injured it could be taken to
a local wildlife sanctuary. Alternatively, if it's an
escaped python, you're just curious. Wounded
animals have a tendency to lash out at anyone
trying to touch them. An exploratory poke with
your walking stick from a safe distance is far better
than a trip to the doctor for a rabies injection.

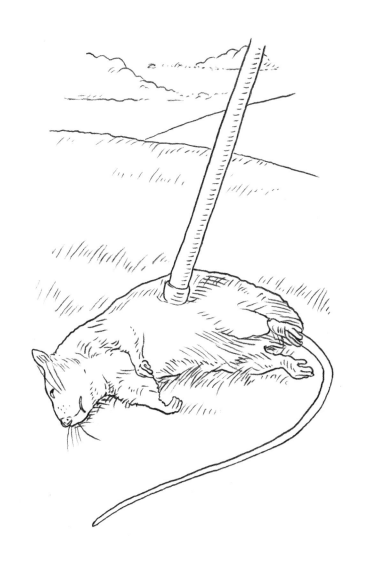

Canal dredger

Back in 2018 the Swedes invented a new exercise
discipline which involved picking up litter
while out for a run. It was called 'plogging', a
combination of the Swedish for 'picking' and
'jogging', which sounds suspiciously like a shelving
insert for an IKEA storage solution. But you don't
need to be super-fit, Scandinavian or wearing
lycra to help out. Canals and ponds are usually
the last resting places of supermarket trolleys,
plastic crates, plastic bags and old shoes. Used
in the reverse position a walking stick is ideal
for hooking out sundry objects that have ended
up in the water and, in the absence of any kind
of current, would remain there. Your good deed
may not have the emotional appeal of freeing a
struggling young turtle from a raft of discarded
plastic but you will be making waterways a safer
place for newts, toads and little ducklings.

Carpet beater

In the olden days – and we mean the proper olden days, not the time when cars came with cassette players – carpets were never fitted. They only ever went up to a foot from the skirting board. Back then vacuum cleaners had all the suck of an asthmatic elephant, so the only way to clean carpets was to 'give 'em a right proper bash' on the clothes line. Fast-forward to this century and the same procedure can be followed to give your Andalusian seagrass hall runner a good going over. Specialist rug beaters are a waste of money when you have a sturdy tool to hand that can do the job.

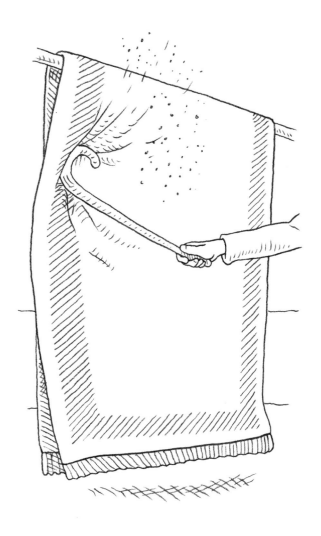

Water disperser

After a deluge or sudden downpour, rainwater can accumulate in many annoying places. Water that builds up in awnings or the edges of a gazebo can stretch the fabric and also encourage the reproduction of mosquitoes. Thus a swift and effective removal of the standing water is of benefit to everyone. A quick solution is to give a sharp upward prod with the walking stick, held in either standard position (with hand on handle) or the reverse position (using the handle end to prod the aqueous bulk). The latter technique is advisable when the fabric holding the water looks to be in less than prime condition and a jab with the sharp end of a walking stick might poke a hole in it. Warning people in the immediate vicinity is optional, depending on how much they annoy you.

Spider relocation tool

Charlotte's Web did a lot for spider PR but sadly not enough. Despite their good deeds in getting rid of irritating flies, their presence often upsets people. Even though a spider's chosen method of dispatching victims is by wrapping them in silk and injecting them with poison, that hardly gives us the moral high ground to bash them with a shoe. Fortunately a walking stick is a good way of coaxing them to relocate. Should the spider be amenable to transferring to the tip of the walking stick, then it can be physically moved outside. If the spider is willing to climb aboard, it is essential that the stick holder is prepared for the spider to run down the stick towards them. It's hard to convince a young person that spiders aren't scary if you've hurled your stick in the air the moment the eight-legged creature runs towards you, eager to make friends.

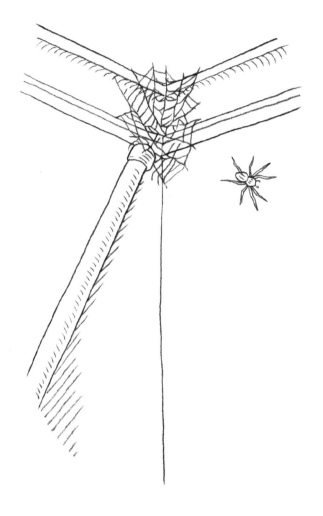

Shelfie stick

A walking stick can be turned into a handy
'shelfie stick' in seconds. Held in the reverse
position and extended upwards, it can hook an
item that is just out of reach on a high shelf.
Depending on the physical robustness of the item,
this can be hooked or alternatively eased gently
towards the edge. Some items, such as an antique
vase, a plant or perhaps a classic old Beatles
record, should be approached with prudence. In
actual fact 'shelfie stick' is not as accurate a term
as 'reachie stick', because they can be employed
to reach (or, if you're American, 'reach out') for
many inaccessible items around the home. They
are very handy for fishing out an errant shoe from
under the bed, a dropped Malteser that has shot
under the settee (the natural refuge for a dropped
Malteser) or, *in extremis*, the spare loo roll.

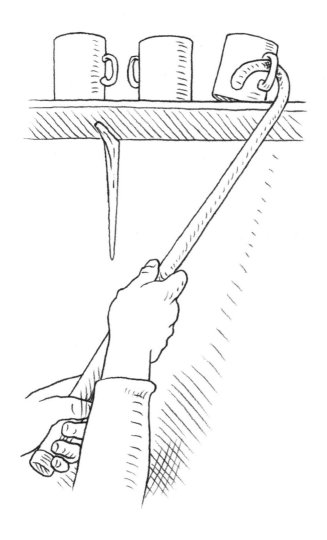

Clothes hanger

Blue Peter presenters were forever showing viewers how to make clothes hangers into something else, so it feels counter-intuitive to make something else into a clothes hanger. The inspiration for this use of a walking stick comes from trendy high-street T-shirt shops which firmly believe that £9.99 isn't the price-point ceiling for a simple white T-shirt with some artless blob of colour or agitprop slogan on the front. They display their overpriced wares on long poles, but a walking stick will happily accommodate one shirt if required. And it often is required when visiting hotels. Despite photos on the website showing each room with a wardrobe capable of holding an entire spring collection, look inside and there are four clothes hangers, three of which have already been purloined by your travel companion.

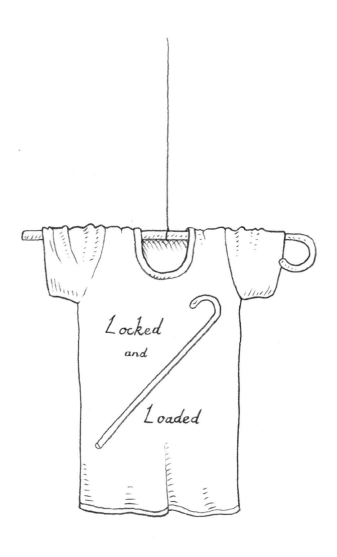

Burglar alarm

There are many sophisticated devices that can be installed in the modern home to prevent burglaries, but an expertly placed walking stick can be just as effective.* A burglar relies on stealth and silence to carry out his vile trade during the hours of darkness, so a crafty trip hazard set at a low height can catch him unawares. Propped in a doorway or narrow passageway with a wood or linoleum flooring, the sudden noise of a walking stick being clattered to the floor is not only an audible signal to the householder that things are amiss downstairs, it is an alarming jolt for the burglar that discovery is imminent, forcing him to flee.

---

* Insurers are unlikely to reduce your insurance premium as a result of installing this device.

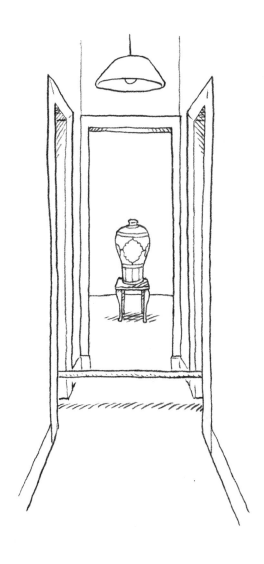

Gutter clearance tool

Global warming affects us all. These days a sudden downpour is more likely to be a sudden deluge, with rain cascading off the roof in monsoon-like volumes. In this scenario it's important to channel the rain through the necessary conduits as quickly as possible. The last thing anyone needs is a gutter blocked with leaves, acorns or a dead squirrel. None of the DIY stores sell impromptu gutter clearance devices, but a walking stick can be quickly and easily hooked over the top of a gutter and run along to the downpipe to allow free passage of water and prevent spillage at unwanted locations along the length.

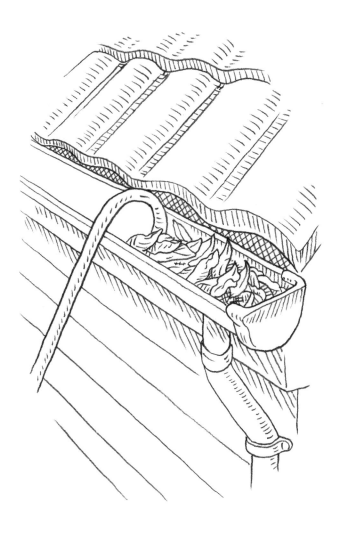

Door prop

Many things can be used to prop open a door, but a walking stick has physics on its side in its claim to be one of the most reliable methods. Using Newton's laws of motion we can postulate that the force aiming to slam the door shut – the wind, or draught – can easily overcome the mass times the gravity of a fairly large object placed against it. Similarly, the coefficent of friction of a wedge jammed under the door may not be enough to resist the applied exterior force, especially if the hall floor has been polished. However, with a walking stick propping the door open, the force needed to compress and break the stick would require many more joules of energy, perhaps a wind of storm force 10. And if that were the case, nobody would want to have the door open anyway.

Back scratcher

We have all seen humorous images from wildlife programmes of grizzly bears rubbing their backs against the bark of a forest tree to relieve an itch. Humans are more dextrous than our ursine cousins and rarely need to resort to a tree. We can reach most parts of our body to respond to the itch with a twist of the shoulder. However, as age takes hold, those rotator cuffs don't rotate as easily as they did before and it's useful to have an extension of the hand to administer the perfect scratch. This is where a walking stick comes in beautifully, as it is a great deal harder than the human hand and indeed you can emulate that bristlecone pine beloved of the grizzly.

Note: There are specialist back scratchers available on the market, but could you clear a gutter or lever up a rock with one?

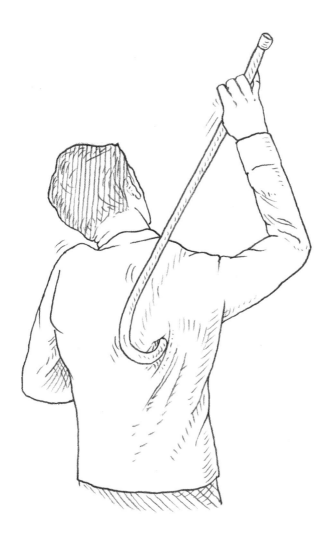

Map pointer

It's difficult not to think of old war movies starring Jack Hawkins when using a great big pointer on a map. Maps and walking in the wrong direction go hand in hand, so when one visits a country park and there is a large-scale map in the car park, a walking stick will help reduce any ambiguity. The exact route you intend to take can be traced with the aid of the improvised pointer, so no one is in any doubt of the proposed direction of travel. Lively discussions can then take place as to whether this is the best route, but at least you are able to have these before you start off, rather than once you've headed off down the wrong path. The stick can also be used to highlight points of interest along the route, before getting to work as the 50th use, a walking stick.

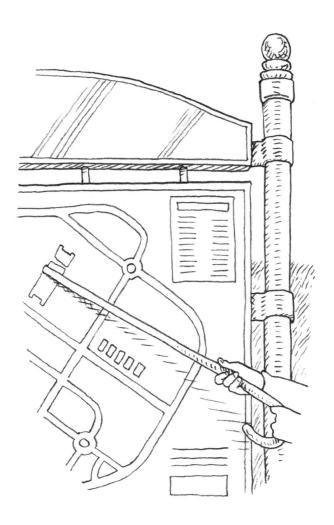

Position locator

It's easy to get lost in a crowd. And it can be a frightening experience if you lose contact with companions in a crowded place you don't know well, with people jostling you left, right and centre. However, if you are equipped with a walking stick you have a personal beacon by your side. A swift wave aloft of the walking stick will immediately establish your position and guide your friends towards you. Or alternatively, it will alert your position to them should they wish to go off in completely the opposite direction. (Why do you think they lost contact with you in the first place? There are only so many fascinating quotes from Nikolaus Pevsner you can listen to.) Perhaps if you often lose touch with a walking companion you could develop a signature flourish to verify your identity above a sea of heads.

Annoyance alert

Shaking a stick at something as a symbol of annoyance has been with us since ancient man first tried to stop a woolly mammoth from parking in front of his cave – which was in constant use. But just as with sign language, a gesture is not enough – there needs to be an accompanying facial expression. The shaking needs to be coupled with a snarl or glower. It is a warning rather than an intention. And a walking stick is the perfect item to shake, because it is an empty threat. The instances of actual assault or GBH involving a walking stick are rare. Should the stick being shaken resemble a cudgel or baseball bat, then that is another thing entirely. Shaking a walking stick also allows the injured party to show annoyance at a distance, when a gesticulating fist could be mistaken for a friendly wave.

Crazy golf putter

Crazy golf putters are typically the hammerhead type. Pick one up and it feels like it was put together by a 12-year-old in a metalwork class; the clubhead usually has independent movement from the shaft, that is, if it stays on for the entire 18 holes. They have not lived happy lives, never felt the loving embrace of a golf bag or nestled in the boot of a top-range Jaguar. Most of their existence has been spent in the hands of small children smashing them into concrete because the ball didn't go through the clown's mouth when they wanted. A walking stick can easily replicate a crazy golf putter, being the perfect shape for it. They can be used on official crazy golf courses or used off-piste in the park with a conker for a ball and uncollected ordure as the target. In that instance, one hole is usually enough.

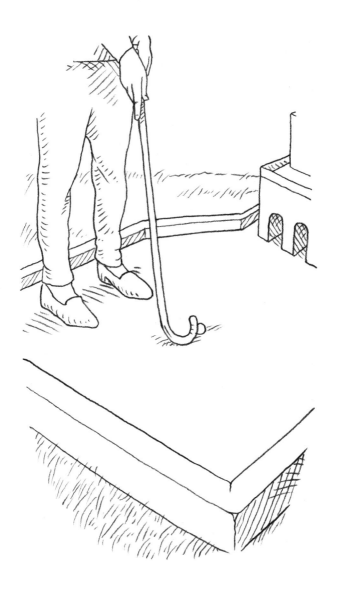

Boat hook

If you are on a canal trip, there's no need to worry with this application of the walking stick – you've probably got a couple of sturdy 5-foot poles on board already, given the regular boat-to-boat contact you'll get. The walking stick as boat hook is best used with that twin-propulsion, shallow-drafting pleasure craft known as the pedalo. It is not the most stable of vessels. The critical moment in any voyage is when the seafarer hoves into port and wants to come ashore. A step towards the landing stage propels the lightweight saucy ship backwards in the opposite direction. So a handy grab for shore with the walking stick will prevent a man overboard. Alternatively, throw it to a helpful person on land who can haul you in without a wobbly challenge to Newton's third law of motion.

Sound generator

As a child, one of your great pleasures was to take a stick and run it along iron railings to see if it would make a glorious clanging sound. Ah yes, those were the days – when the phones you had were at the corner of the street in red telephone boxes, not in every child's pocket. You can still take your walking stick and run it along those railings, but it won't be at quite the same speed and you may need your inhaler afterwards. Indeed, a walking stick can be used to produce all kinds of marvellous sounds. Struck sharply against the side of large metal objects it can act like the clapper of a bell. Or it produces the sound of grand timpani when whacked on the top of an empty wheelie bin, very much like *Last of the Summer Wine* meets *Stomp*.

Tent peg

The first law of camping is that you never return with the same amount of tent pegs that you started out with. Tent pegs have a high mortality rate. They get vigorously hammered into the earth when pitching the tent, yet in the rush to pack up and beat the impending rain at the end of the stay, a straggler or two will be left behind. Some simply won't budge once planted in the ground. Some accept a couple of lusty blows from a mallet then bend sideways with the next two wallops and refuse to be straightened ever again. A walking stick carefully inserted into the ground will make a worthy substitute for a missing tent peg, especially as the lead peg holding the guy rope. Also, having your personal stick as your lead peg makes identifying your tent in a field of homogenous canvas much easier.

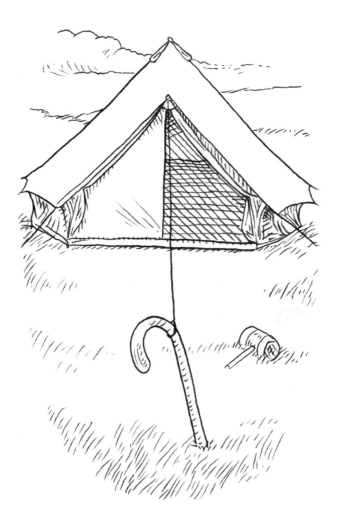

Mooring post

The British love messing about in boats, from Ratty and Moley to Sir Steve and Sir Matthew. And who can forget that halcyon trip up the River Thames portrayed by Jerome K. Jerome in *Three Men in a Boat*? The best places to moor up of an evening are the quiet stretches of empty riverbank where you can be alone with nature, the stars and the river. Not surprisingly, these don't come equipped with mooring hooks. But there's no need to give up your chosen spot for want of a place to tie on. It's a simple task to hop ashore with a walking stick, drive it hard into the ground and then affix the mooring rope with a double bowline, rolling half-hitch cleat knot with a round turn thrown in for good measure. Or better still, have a rope with a loop on the end.

Orchestra baton

Classical music takes hold of us and makes us do unexpected things. Take the Last Night of the Proms, when the front five rows are filled with the kind of people you would never wish to meet on holiday. Released into the community for one night only, they make their way to the Albert Hall dressed as Britannia and John Bull and proceed to conduct the orchestra along with the professional conductor, easily distinguished by his white tuxedo and his ability to keep time. A walking stick can be used to emulate the maestro at those moments of sheer bliss, though given its weight, the impromptu conducting is unlikely to go on for a whole movement. In fact it is likely to last only a few bars before someone is struck around the ear or it gets too heavy.

Fender Stratocaster

In the pantheon of rock gods there are very few
bass guitarists – kids grow up wanting to be Jimi
Hendrix, Eric Clapton, Jeff Beck or Brian May.
There are those like Springsteen and Richards
who prefer the Fender Telecaster, but the best-
known instrument of the guitar hero is the Fender
Stratocaster, used so brilliantly by David Gilmour
on many soaring Pink Floyd guitar solos. When
the volume is turned up to 11 for that plangent,
swooping sound, it is second nature to reach for
a guitar substitute and mime along with those
moments of pure ecstasy. Tennis rackets are never
to hand, and air guitars are frankly embarrassing
– however, with a walking stick strapped on and
plugged in, you can run your hand down the
fretboard while picking out notes on the body and
dreaming of the time you had Robert Plant's hair
and Jimmy Page's trousers.

Pooh stick

He may have been a Bear of Very Little Brain, but he invented a game that is played throughout the world, with the exception of mainland China. Poohsticks, as devised by Winnie the Pooh, involves each player dropping a stick from a bridge into a flowing stream beneath and seeing which comes out first the other side. Except when the residents of Hundred Acre Wood play it and Eeyore comes floating out the other side. It is best to use sticks or twigs found nearby, but *in extremis*, one can join in by lobbing a walking stick into the current to see how it fares against more natural items. This can be very expensive if you don't have an eager Jack Russell to dive into the stream and retrieve it afterwards.

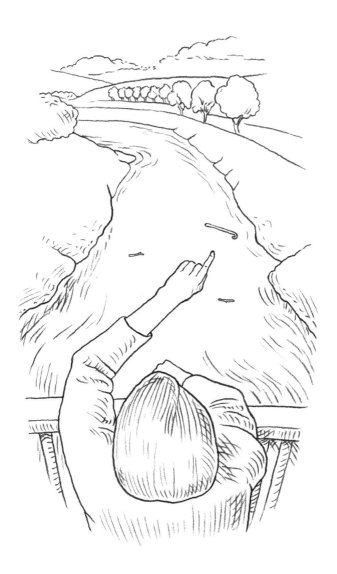

Bird scarer

Pigeons are a menace to most garden vegetable patches, which they view as an all-you-can-eat buffet. When they are not chomping on cabbages, sprouts, kale, cauliflowers and peas, they'll turn their attention to newly sewn grass. Rabbits and squirrels can be just as destructive, but they tend to be frightened off by the merest sudden noise. Pigeons hold their nerve a lot longer. They are far more difficult to get rid of at a distance and need a grand theatrical gesture, such as the waving of a large stick at them in a random fashion. Close to hand, a walking stick is the perfect aid for an angry gardener charging down the garden to rescue their crop; if frustration gets the better of them, it can be hurled, too.

Plant support

While out strolling along a busy border, one can often spot a sagging sambucus or a drooping delphinium. Left unattended, the unsupported stem can easily fold over and break in the mildest of winds. However, swift intervention with a walking stick can make all the difference to maintaining the plant's perfect form. Used as a handy plant support it will give all the necessary rigidity until a more garden-appropriate stake, such as a bamboo cane or wire hoop, can be installed to preserve your border display.

Toad nudger

If the grass in your garden gets on the 'meadowy' side, necessitating a cut on the mower's loftiest height setting, then a walking stick is a handy tool to carry on board. Long grass often encourages a variety of fauna and, in the dampest of spots, it's possible to find young amphibians lurking. Oblivious of the impending consequences of an inopportune hop at the wrong moment, the frog or toad should be encouraged to move before the deadly blades pass overhead. A friendly tap with a walking stick, directing them to the mown side of the garden, will avert this catastrophe. You can leave slugs where they are. They had it coming.

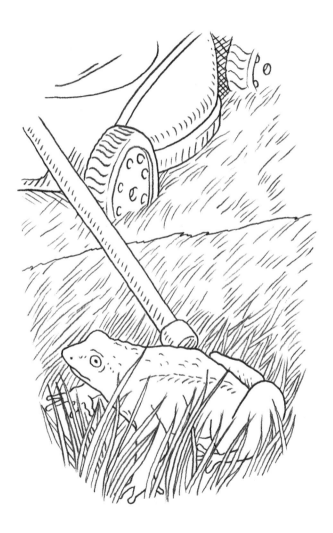

Dibber

Granted, a few of the 49 uses of a walking stick contained within this guide might be deemed a less than satisfactory substitute for the real thing, but a walking stick employed as a dibber is almost as good as the genuine article. In some instances it is better. A dibber is a short wooden spike which is pressed into the earth to make an adequate hole into which an individual seed is then popped – it comes into its own when used in the outdoor seedbed. It can also be used to make wider apertures to drop in bulbs, seedlings or plug plants when planting out. A walking stick used to facilitate this process can be employed without the gardener bending over or getting down onto troublesome knee joints. Although administration of the seed *will* inevitably oblige a trip to soil level.

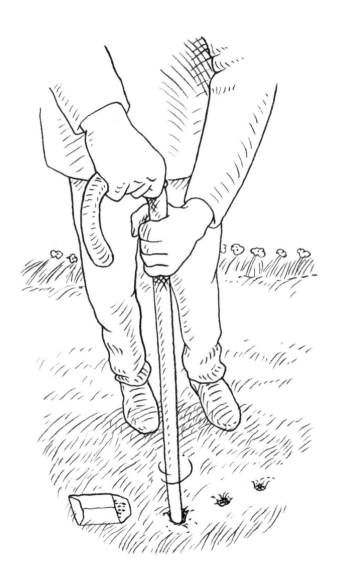

Slug flicker

Even when wearing gloves there are some things you don't want to pick up with your hands in the garden: dead mice, 'messages' left by foxes, unexploded munitions and, worst of all, slugs. Slugs are a difficult subject for gardening programmes because they hedge around the subject of bumping them off. While the majority of gardeners simply spread out large quantities of deadly blue pellets, television programmes would sooner gardeners repel them by surrounding plants with wool. A halfway house between these two approaches is to flick them into an open space or neighbour's garden where they might be eaten by a predator. A walking stick makes a perfect slug flicker. It is light, eminently portable and the perfect length for a wrist flick. It also appeals to the British sense of fair play – this way the slugs get a fighting chance.

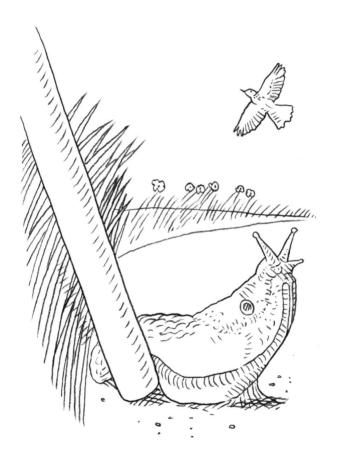

Dog entertainment centre

It is a truth universally acknowledged that a dog is never happier than when it has got a stick in its mouth. Surprisingly small dogs like surprisingly large sticks, which is probably the canine extension of small man/flash car syndrome. To save your dog the bother of going out and rootling around in the hedgerow to drag out a stick, give them a walking stick. Dogs often pick up cuts or gouges to their mouths from the rough spurs and knobbles on the side of wild sticks, so this will prevent injuries too. Yes, there will be a few teethmarks along the shaft of your walking stick, but it's a small price to pay.

Dog stirrer

Installed in front of a glowing fire on a winter's evening, dogs know they are a lot better off than in the perishingly cold kitchen where their basket resides, and so will carefully ignore a coaxing 'come on'. The walking stick can be deftly employed as a humane way to move them on. First of all the concept of their imminent departure can be introduced by a gentle little scratch between the ears, followed by a tender little prod when they open their eyes. The scale and pressure of this contact can be increased until sooner or later they accept the inevitable and move on with no long-term hard feelings. Should you come across an animal blocking the road in a safari park, this technique can also be deployed, but remember to take out comprehensive insurance before you go.

Dog parking

Although dogs are accepted in many businesses and venues, occasionally they need to be tied up outside. Shops will often have convenient places to tie up a dog and your average high street has so much road furniture that you could secure an entire dogs' home in the space of 50 yards. An alternative is to bury a walking stick into the ground as a kind of temporary hitching post and attach the dog lead. The depth of the insertion of the walking stick will depend on how likely it is that your dog will make a bolt for it and also the size of your dog.

Dog lead

A walking stick can be pressed into service as an emergency dog lead should the need arise. It has its drawbacks, but then again so do space-saver wheels. Just as a space-saver wheel will get you and your car home safely, the walking stick will get you and an exuberant dog home safely. Hooked around the dog's collar it can restrain them when there is a danger they might run into traffic or chase off after another dog. It is also much better for the owner's lumber vertebrae than bending down and holding on to the collar for any length of time. It is inadvisable to use with a Chihuahua or Great Dane for obvious reasons, but if attempted, please record the event and upload it to YouTube.

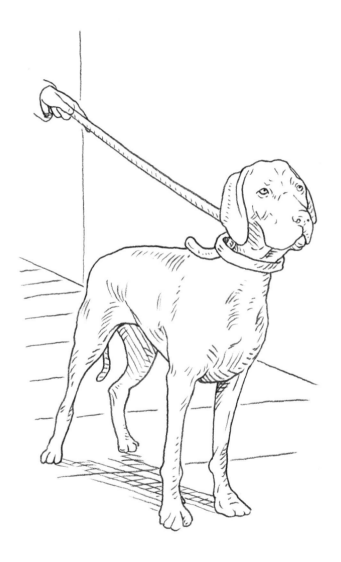

Tide direction indicator

There's so much to organise and occupy yourself with on a trip to the beach that it's hard to work out whether the tide is coming in or going out. If it's a wide beach, with no points of reference, it's even more difficult. One solution is to take a walking stick and plant it firmly in the sand 20 yards from the water's edge. Return 15 minutes later and if the sea is further away it's going out; if it's closer, then the tide is coming in; if it's about the same, the tide is on the turn; and if it's already underwater you will need to move your stuff a lot further up the beach ...

Sand inscriber

Before there was Facebook and Twitter, there was the medium of the beach. A vast stretch of firm wet sand is an open invitation to write something personal for public consumption; and, just like Facebook, it will be washed over and forgotten in about 12 hours. The problem is, there's nothing to write with ... unless you have brought along a walking stick. A walking stick is the perfect tool for the job; lightweight and the ideal length, it can be used for pictures and messages, or alternatively to mark out the lines of impromptu football pitches and tennis courts. Sticks are so useful it's surprising that art materials shops don't stock them.

Flagpole

One of the great joys of a visit to the beach is the opportunity to build sandcastles – or, if you want to take the liberal, non-martial approach – sand affordable housing. They can become sizeable projects. Once the ramparts are fortified, the moats dug, the tricky arch (which collapsed three times before you got it right) built and the turrets placed on each corner, what you need to top it off is a majestic flagpole. A walking stick will make a worthy staff on which to unfurl the Union Jack and claim this bold fortification for Blighty.

Back to Base, base

The childhood game of Back to Base is known by many different names: 123 Home, Forty-Forty, Blocky 123, 44 Home and Mob Mob. For those unfamiliar with the concept, it's like Hide and Seek except the seeker, or 'It', has to seek out those that are hiding and when they are discovered run back to touch the base before the hiders can get there first. At the same time, other hiders can sneak back to the base and claim immunity. The chosen base is often a tree or lamppost. However, using a walking stick driven into the ground as the base has tremendous advantages, because a location can be chosen which is the perfect distance from an array of different hiding places, balancing cover and open ground, safety and jeopardy.

Wheel of fortune

Faced with a difficult decision, there are many ways to let fate intervene in your choice. You can roll the dice or toss a coin. If you're arguing as to whose turn it is, you can cut cards, play Rock, Paper, Scissors or Spoof. With a walking stick at hand there is another option – spinning the wheel of fortune. The hedonistic thrill of chance can be yours providing you find a frictionless surface on which to spin the stick, and ideally a fulcrum on which it can more easily rotate. Like those spin-the-bottle moments from teenage years, you can let the stick decide your fate. So next time your coastal walking group gets into a debate about whose turn it is to pay the parking charge, spin the wheel of fortune. It's more Vegas than Ventnor.

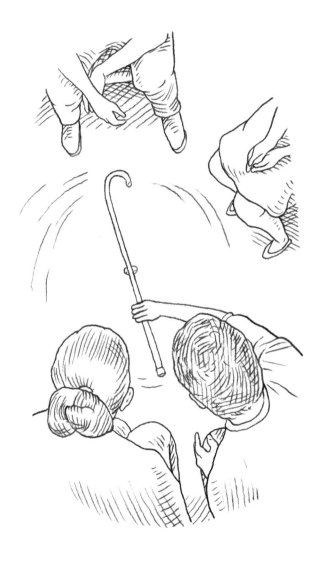

Upstairs noise abater

It might have shades of the sitcom stereotype, but banging a walking stick on the ceiling to get upstairs to quieten down is sometimes necessary. You could use a broom handle, but walking sticks are easier. It's best to do it with the handle end unless you want to create a unique fresco in your ceiling plaster – save the sharp end for banging on the floor to get downstairs to shut up. The international signal of discontent is three evenly spaced knocks. Two is too few and could be the work of some mechanical device clicking in; four is too many and could be a hammer at work. Of course, the nightmare scenario is that upstairs has been rented out as an Airbnb and the occupants don't give a darn about making too much noise. And if you live in a normal detached house, that's even more worrying.

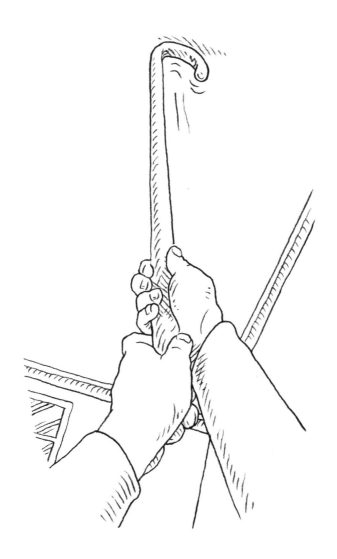

No entry barrier

Rarely does a day pass when the owner of a walking stick does not feel like recreating the classic scene from *Lord of the Rings*, where, on the Bridge of Khazad-dûm, Gandalf makes a stand against the marauding, fire-breathing Balrog. Facing imminent destruction, Gandalf turns to face the creature, slams his staff into the bridge and shouts. 'You cannot pass ... Go back to the Shadow!' It is a bit over the top to say that to someone jumping the queue in the Co-op, but a swift strategic positioning of the walking stick will certainly help. A walking stick makes a great impromptu barrier, whether it's preventing a toddler from running out onto the road, herding chickens, or stopping lippy teenagers from jumping the queue. The last two examples being very much the same.

Remote button presser

Sometimes you need to press a button or flick a switch and you just cannot get to it, like being jammed in a lift and not wanting to ask someone to press your floor button. If it's a crowded lift, a surreptitious reach-round could end in embarrassing consequences if the lift jolts or comes to a shuddering halt. Much better to avoid any kind of hand-to-stranger contact by making a firm jab with a walking stick. Walking sticks also come in handy in flicking switches that are out of reach, particularly in lofts and garages. Men are natural hoarders and garages are responsible, giving them somewhere to dump everything that might-come-in-useful-one-day. Hence garages become jam-packed and to turn the light on you have to take a walking stick, wedge your arm against the wall and thread it behind a series of boxes to flick the switch.

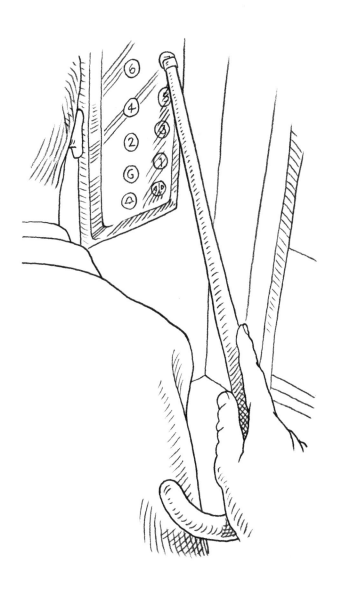

Crowd divider

We cannot be 100 per cent certain that Moses
did not part the Red Sea with a walking stick.
According to the Book of Exodus, Moses held
out his 'staff' towards the body of water and God
parted the Red Sea – staff, walking stick, what's
the difference? What we can say for certain is that
a modern, non-biblical walking stick is good for
steering your way through and parting a crowd.
Hold the handle end out in front of you and the
stick at arm's length and set off resolutely in that
direction. Not only does it clear people out of
the way, it sends a firm signal of your direction
of travel. If you are leading a fair-sized group
of people, you can also use the walking stick to
telegraph a left or right turn, very much like a
bandleader with a marching band.

Role play

For the budding amateur thespian, a walking stick is the ultimate prop for improvisation. Indeed, following the publication of this book, the author's agent will be engaged in selling the stage rights for a performance at the Edinburgh Fringe: *49 Uses of a Walking Stick* – the great one-man, one-prop show. It can be ...

- A *Star Wars* lightsaber
- Zorro's flashing blade
- A stave for the friendly fight between Robin Hood and Little John
- The axe wielded by Jack Nicholson in *The Shining*
- The cudgel used by Bill Sikes in *Oliver!*
- Dick van Dyke's 'Me Ol' Bamboo' in *Chitty Chitty Bang Bang*
- A wizarding wand for Harry, Ron, and Hermione, but particularly Dumbledore
- A sentry's rifle for presenting arms outside Buckingham Palace
- A snorkel
- A periscope
- A fishing rod
- A saxophone
- A trombone slide
- Edward's scissorhands
- The bottom half of Mary Poppins' umbrella

Emergency splint

One of the quirks of life is that you never break an arm or a leg when you are expecting to. Not unless you regularly attempt to jump a motorbike over 14 double-decker buses. The sudden fracture of a limb is a shock both in the statistical and the medical sense. Assistance is needed immediately. It hurts like crazy and the injury needs stabilising or further damage can be done. A walking stick bound tightly against the injured limb makes the perfect stand-in splint until the emergency services arrive on the scene with a more tailored solution. Should you break two arms at once and are helped out by the provision of two walking sticks, make sure your friends don't take a photo of you and post it on social media as a scarecrow.

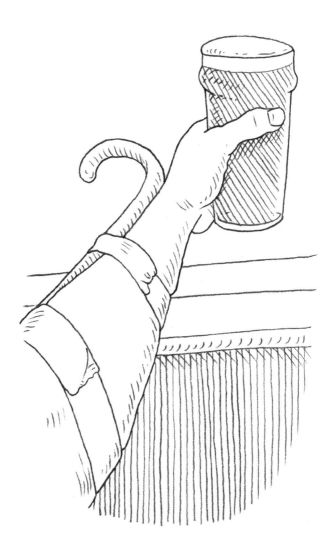

Low-tech compass

There's a touch of the Bear Grylls in all of us. That is why wilderness survival programmes are so popular on television despite the fact that we have no Kalahari Desert or Yosemite National Park. We like the vicarious thrill of wondering what we would do if every GPS device we owned went kaput. A walking stick will help: planted in the ground, the shadow it casts at noon will point north, so to the left is west, to the right is east. If it isn't midday, you can place a stone at the tip of the shadow, wait for half an hour, then place another stone at the tip of where the shadow has moved to. A line drawn between these two stones will give you the rough line of east–west. You can rest assured that should you become hopelessly lost the sun will always be shining.

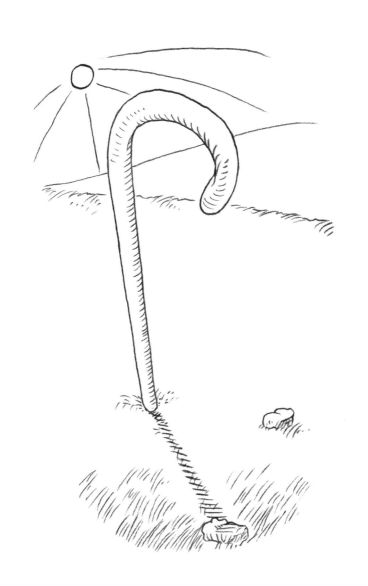

In-flight knee protector

Flying can be a stressful experience at the best of times, but it is made worse by the person in front lowering their seat on top of you the moment the free drinks have disappeared. On long-haul flights it is inevitable that people will want to lever the seat back and snooze, but some people choose to do it whatever the length of flight. A crafty little tip is to jam a walking stick between your seat and the seatback in front to prevent it from reclining and banging into your knees. Should the flight attendant be called, explain that you have just had your knee replaced and the seat in front is impacting it. They are unlikely to demand an inspection of the scar, and the walking stick you have is ample verification that you have a poorly knee. Indeed, you should probably be upgraded.

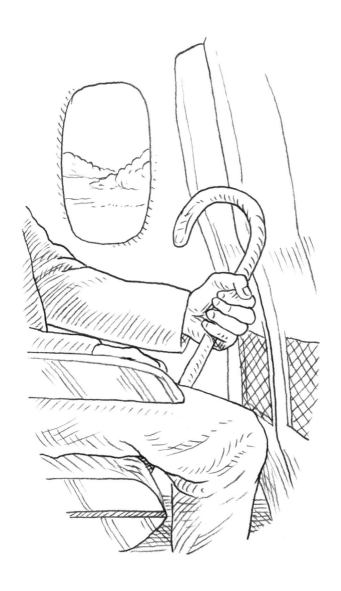

Balancing aid

A walking stick makes a great balancing aid.
That doesn't mean to say you are fully equipped
to attempt a high-wire act because you have one,
just as owning a gold lamé leotard doesn't turn
you into a trapeze artist. However, a walking stick
extended to the side can be a useful balancing aid
while walking along a low wall or across a series
of stepping stones in a river. If this latter is the
case, to be honest keeping your eyes open for
the slippery, moss-covered patches on the rocks
is probably more important than waving a stick
around. Though it will help you lever yourself up
off the river bed.

Further uses of a walking stick

If you find that 49 uses of a walking stick aren't enough, and are worried that you might actually have to start walking with the damned thing, here are a few more we couldn't quite squeeze in:

- To beat a piñata – a piñata stuffed with Werther's Originals would certainly liven up the McCarthy & Stone residents' Christmas party.

- A zombie barrier – it is a well-known fact that zombies can't lift their feet more than 4 inches off the ground; a walking stick propped a foot above the floor will stop the blighters.

- To prop open sash windows, cold frames or car bonnets.

- The walking stick is a great general pointer. An extended arm is nowhere near as precise as the rifle-barrel accuracy of an extended arm holding a stick.

- To indicate to your companions your position in a maze. (NB, it must be quite a low maze.)

- Instant Captain Hook impersonation – pull down your sleeve to cover your hand, insert stick up sleeve until only top is visible and voila!

- Anchoring a kite on windswept afternoons while you reach for the Thermos/hip flask.